Children in our World

RACISM AND INTOLERANCE

Louise Spilsbury

Hanane Kai

WAYLAND

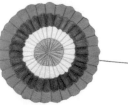

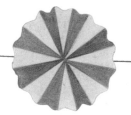

Published in paperback in Great Britain in 2018 by Wayland

Text © Hodder and Stoughton, 2017
Written by Louise Spilsbury
Illustrations © Hanane Kai, 2017

Texturing of illustrations by Sarah Habli
Edited by Corinne Lucas
Designed by Sophie Wilkins

A catalogue for this title is available from the British Library.
ISBN: 978 1 5263 0053 9
10 9 8 7 6 5 4 3 2 1

FSC
www.fsc.org
MIX
Paper from
responsible sources
FSC® C104740

Printed in China

Wayland
An imprint of
Hachette Children's Books
Part of Hodder & Stoughton
Carmelite House
50 Victoria Embankment
London, EC4Y 0DZ

An Hachette UK Company
www.hachette.co.uk
www.hachettechildrens.co.uk

Contents

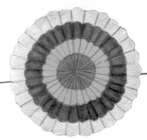

The world is made up of all sorts of people. We like different foods, play different sports and have different hobbies. Most of us live happily side by side. We get to know each other and act with kindness and respect.

Sadly, some people do not always treat others fairly. They may be very unkind to people they think are different to them.

5

Sometimes people are treated differently because of the colour of their skin, their family background or the country they come from. This is known as racism.

Racism is a form of prejudice. Prejudice is when someone dislikes anyone from a particular group of people, without knowing them. Imagine disliking someone before you have spoken to them or know anything about them. Does that sound fair?

Some people are intolerant of those who live a different way of life to them. Intolerance is when people do not accept someone else's family, home, religion or lifestyle because it is different to theirs.

PRIORITY SEATING
FOR ELDERLY
AND DISABLED

Intolerance can take many forms. One kind is when people speak badly of other people's religion, or treat people from a different religion unfairly. Everyone should be able to follow the faith they choose, without being hated.

PRIORITY SEATING
FOR ELDERLY
AND DISABLED

People can become prejudiced when one person from a group does something bad or wrong. They start to believe that everyone from that group is bad, even though that is not fair or true.

Sometimes people are unkind to anyone who looks or acts differently to them. Even if you disagree with someone's beliefs, you should still respect their way of life.

At school, a pupil might make a joke about another person's religion. They may call someone a nasty name or leave them out of a game because they speak another language or look different to them.

Being treated differently because of your race or religion is never funny or fair. It can make people feel alone, angry and scared. Some children may be too upset to concentrate in class or to go to school. It can even make them ill.

People who are racist and intolerant may shout at, threaten or hurt other people. They might paint bad words on people's homes or places of worship, or even bomb buildings.

Some people are told they cannot live in certain places or do certain jobs, or they may be paid less money because of the colour of their skin or their beliefs. They may be told they cannot wear certain clothes. How would you feel if that happened to you?

Racism and intolerance create a world where people do not trust and respect each other. They stir up bad feelings and hatred. This hatred can cause fighting and lead to wars.

Some people are killed because of their race or their religion.
Families are forced to leave their homes. They try to escape
to a new place where they hope to be able to live in safety
and peace.

Many people across the world work hard to stop racism and intolerance. Countries have laws to stop people being refused jobs or treated unfairly.

A charity is a group that helps people. Some charity workers help people affected by racism and intolerance to get fair treatment. They try to teach people why racism and intolerance are wrong, what problems these things cause and the harm they do.

Rules keep us safe. Schools have strict rules about racism. In some countries, schools keep records of any racist bullying that happens. Teachers have steps to follow if a pupil is treated unfairly because of racism or intolerance.

The police can take action to protect people from racism and intolerance, too. They can make reports about people who shout angry insults or hurt others. They can even arrest and imprison them.

Tolerance means respecting others for their differences. We are all different from each other in some way. You might not think the way you look or do things is different or unusual because you are used to them. But we all must appear different to others.

Differences are what make the world an interesting place. If someone at your school comes from another country, why not ask them about it? To learn about other beliefs, perhaps you could invite a friend to celebrate one of your festivals and share in one of theirs.

We are all much more alike than we are different. We all need food, water, clothes and a home to live in. We all need to learn, work and have fun in our lives. We all laugh, cry, and like to spend time with our family and friends. We all need to be free and safe.

When you meet someone new try to find things you have in common, as well as respecting differences. Do you like the same subjects at school? Do you like the same music, jokes, games, or films? Finding the things that connect us can be fun.

Racism and intolerance make a lot of people angry and upset.
If you feel worried or sad, talk to a parent or an adult you trust.
They can help you to feel better. If you have been
bullied because of your race, culture or beliefs,
tell an adult straight away.

Racism and intolerance are wrong and unfair. But remember, there
are many people, of all races and religions, working to make things
better. Most people around the world are tolerant and caring.

You can help change attitudes by learning about other cultures and religions. If you see someone being treated badly or unfairly because of their race or culture, check they are OK and tell an adult you trust.

You could also sell old toys or put on a show to raise money for charities and groups that work to stop racism and intolerance. Or you could help your teacher to arrange a world culture day at school.

Find Out More

If you are a victim of racism or intolerance, it is very important that you tell an adult you trust about how you are being treated. You can also contact Childline for support on any issue. www.childline.org.uk

Books

Rachel's Story – A Journey from a country in Eurasia
Andy Glynne, Wayland, 2016

We All Come from Different Cultures
Melissa Higgins, Raintree, 2016

Who We Are!: All About Being the Same and Being Different
Robie Harris, Walker Books, 2016

Websites

Show Racism the Red Card is a group that uses top footballers to educate against racism.
www.theredcard.org

Stop Hate UK challenges all forms of discrimination, based on any part of a person's identity.
www.stophateuk.org

Glossary

charity a group that helps people in need

culture the beliefs, values and ways of behaving and celebrating that a particular group of people share

intolerance refusing to accept views, beliefs or behaviours that are different from your own

laws rules that people in a country must follow

prejudice disliking a person or group simply because they belong to a particular race, religion or different group

race a group of people who may come from the same place, share the same language and look similar in some way

religion a belief in a god or gods, for example Islam and Christianity

respect to care about other people's feelings and opinions

tolerance the ability to accept views, ways of life or beliefs that are different from your own

worship to show respect for a god, for example by praying

Index